Visit Marq Mervin online at:
marqmervin.com

Cover by Lawrence Maxwell
Illustrations and layout by Marq Mervin

ISBN: 978-1-7348361-0-3 (pbk.)
ISBN: 978-1-7348361-2-7 (ebook)

Set in Adobe Garamond Pro and Chaparral Pro

One Day, I Hope That...

FOREWARD

Oftentimes, the artist is underappreciated, misunderstood, underpaid, and seen as a hobbyist.

What many fail to realize is the artist has the power to turn the temporary into the timeless, create the tangible and intangible, and transform the ephemeral to eternal. The artist, at the core, is the practitioner of human expression. Through that expression—whether it be happiness, pain, joy, sorrow, or healing—are we all reminded of our humanity.

Each of us is on a journey sailing down the ocean of Time. A journey that we call, Life. We encounter other sailors who are also coasting along this excursion. When we find drifters we're fond of—whether they be friends or lovers—we exchange ropes and tie our boats to one another. This is why they're called relationships. Until our time to part ways comes, I hope to enjoy their company on our voyage. Maybe I'll find the recipient of my heart along the way. Maybe I already have. Regardless, I pray to live long, dream happily, and to allow the universe's love to both fill me and overflow from my vessel into someone else.

To all of my muses—I thank you for your influence and inspiration.

Allow me to etch you into infinity so you may live forever.

Contents

LOVE

LAMENTATION

LIBERATION

To queer boys and queer men,

Look upward to the sky and remember you are still here, beloved.
Our lives are so important. Cool your heart and keep going.
I dedicate my words and thoughts to you.

We have a funny relationship,
you and I...

LOVE

Adam

What the hell did I do?
What is this feeling in my heart?
Did I start liking you?

I knew I would adore you the moment I saw your face. Your eyes spoke to my spirit. It was strange—but I needed it. I needed to feel love. Intimacy, chemistry, connection...the things I've been afraid of. Scared that I would never find again. But I think I wanted you because I needed to know those feelings could exist for me. The desire for love burned deep within me. The fire became much warmer after our rendezvous in my hotel room. I was sad because, much like when I fell in love with my old flame, I met you in a city thousands of miles away. Then, I had to depart.

You didn't resemble him entirely. Rather, you reminded me of what it felt like to be comfortable—vulnerable, perhaps—with another man. You led me to a place I thought disappeared. You brought me to happiness. With you, I felt safe. Damn you...I guarded my heart closely, longing for the day I could lower my barricade. And you, whose eyes were filled with magic and wonder, pierced right into my soul and saw how tired I was. How much I desired protection. How weary I was from the journey of solitude. That's exactly why I wanted you—to remind me of my humanity. I wondered if I reminded you of yours. I also wondered if I should rid myself of those thoughts because I started to *feel* again.

Funny enough, the sink in the bathroom wasn't working. Water filled it up because the stopper wasn't placed properly. But, after you came, you secured the stopper so the water flowed down the drain. Much like the sink that held too much water, my heart held too many emotions. You came and fixed them both.

Thank you, Adam.

Boys

When I was younger, I was infatuated with them. I was also afraid of them. Rather, I was afraid of what my infatuation meant. Was it having friends to play with? Was it discovering my desire for more? Did my thoughts creep into territories a child should not know of? Did I *like* them?

There were many boys. Some were my age, some a year older. I wondered what they thought of me. I wondered if they were curious about kissing… *us* kissing. As we've grown into men, I wonder—if given the opportunity, would we explore intimacy? Would the passion be greater? Almost ferocious and alive because we were doing things we "shouldn't"? Or would it just be "boys being boys"? As I've aged and matured, I've come to accept and embrace my infatuation with men.

There was one boy. I remember his name as clearly as I remember the house I first called home. He was cute in his own way. He wasn't the funniest, but he was an outcast of sorts. At that young age, I knew I wanted him intimately. Sex, to my young mind, was kissing. In my adolescent eyes, intimacy was a hug and inside jokes. I wanted both, but I often pondered— is that what he wanted? And, if he did, would he want that with a Black boy? "He's white, so he wouldn't want you", is what I thought. Many white crushes were for naught, as I felt those white boys, if curious about kissing and hugs, didn't and wouldn't share those experience with a Black boy. For fear of shame and disgust. For desiring something that wasn't *normal* with someone that wasn't *normal*. I wasn't like them, yet, I liked them.

There were many boys when I was a freshman in high school. It felt right because they were brown like me. My infatuation often haunted me and drove me to a silence that protected me from sharing too much too soon. The fears of retaliation, bullying, punishment, and the thought of my deepest secrets brought to a burning light horrified me.

There were three boys in particular. As not to reveal their identities, I will use the monikers *Marcel, Alonzo,* and *Carlos*. Each rented temporary rooms inside my mind.

I admired Marcel. He was a husky kid like myself. Though, he was a few inches taller than me. His skin was smooth and mocha-colored. His lips full, eyebrows bushy, and his choice of cologne was exquisite. I knew him briefly and his stature made me feel a sense of security. A security I longed for in this unknown and aggressive terrain called high school. Nothing came of my hidden admiration. Though, my crush on him taught me that I liked other husky boys.

Alonzo was similar to Marcel, though honey-orange skin glazed this boy who's height was similar to mine. He was a troublemaker. A true renegade with a tumultuous history that I dare not share without his permission. We were polar opposites. However, we shared an affinity for Hip-Hop. While he spoke on topics of a fabricated street life filled with crime, drugs, and violence—much like the music we were exposed to—I professed my love of the art, my experiences, and stories of imagined characters. I liked that. The tail side of the coin as he, rightfully, showed his ass every chance he could. My crush was short-lived, but I learned that I liked the bad boy as well.

Carlos—I remember him fondly. He was much different than Marcel and Alonzo. Carlos was short and much lighter than me. He was slightly chubby with a thick, beautiful afro that reminded me of Bone Thugs-N-Harmony. His spirit bubbled with quirky energy. I wonder if this came from his Cuban heritage. He was fun and creative, with a knack for forming beats that laid the foundation for lunchroom freestyles. I liked him a lot. I wanted to gain his deepest friendship. I hoped it would lead to a kiss and a hug like what I imagined as a younster.

Though, my understanding of sex had expanded in high school. So the thought of touching each other crossed my mind often. However, the single-sided infatuation fizzled out as he changed drastically. His relationship with a girl we both knew prompted him to focus his attention on them. Rightfully so. Though, my feelings were hurt. No longer innocent and full of life, Carlos "matured" past me and our other mutual friends. We all felt that sting. Now, his room in my mind is nothing more than a closed door with aged memories and fantasies layered in dust.

Lips

I'm enamored by your lips
Thick. Full. Your words are like nectar that drips
Slowly. The color of warm amber
Honeycombs form as you craft stanzas.
Is it your intellect that enthralls me?
Much like mine, you've fortified your heart. So, did our walls meet?
Did they crumble upon touch? My eyes are spellbound
By your presence. My senses muddle and now I smell sounds,
I feel flavors, and I desire to taste what I see
If my flesh touches yours, can we exchange the air that we breathe?
As I connect with he, I'm awakened to his three
Our minds play chess and our souls shatter as our bodies meet
Then we, become a unit—a movement
We've broken worlds while the universe howls in amusement
The order and chaos that could ensue from one kiss
I've made peace with my fate when I witnessed your lips

Masc(k)

It's okay to be scared. It's okay to be different. I'm different.

This man has strong warm hands. Massive, as if my head could be cradled in his palm. If he sang, he would be a baritone. Earthy and rough. There's texture there that reminds me of the warm aroma from mahogany when it burns slowly. There's a bite to it.

His shoulders are broad, firm, and assured. His arms carry strength, but aren't overly defined. I gaze at his chest and salivate over the mass that's vaguely hidden underneath his light cotton tee-shirt. I make my way down this ever expanding maze of man until I slowly outline the curves of his belly. Rotund, but solid. His insecurities symmetrically placed on his body. Those sides I wish to hold like handle bars as we make love.

He's wearing dark blue denim jeans, though my mind wanders at the thought of this mountainous being wearing khaki shorts, dark gray slacks, or sweatpants. As I lust for what's underneath, I focus on the legs that support and move this man. Thick tree trunks waiting to be caressed.

The way he walks is immaculate. His core is crafted with fortitude so every movement has weight behind it. He exudes strength as he twists his hips forward for each step. There resides gentle power with explosive potential. His waist is thick…immense…sturdy. Stable, yet flexible, similar to his demeanor. His brown legs have traversed an expansive world. Did he play sports? Does he lift weights? Or maybe this is his natural build with no training, but simply genetics? Whatever the case, he is blessed beyond measure, as are my eyes.

In this moment, I thank God for giving me the breath of life. Thank you God for your grace and handcrafted work through this man. The man I've only seen once, yet want to navigate my future with. The man who's team I can support. I see You in him. At least, I want to, but something is…off.

His aura feels strangely familiar to me. It feels peculiar. You know, "different". The kind of "different" where I've had to remind myself, "it's okay to be this way". I wonder if the qualities I find most attractive are the sources of his insecurities. The hands I crave to grasp once held the pieces of many broken hearts, including his own. The wounds and battle scars are invisible to sight but perfectly clear to insight. Is he fearful to hold my heart because he's trying his damnedest to keep his together?

His wide shoulders are, unsurprisingly, tense. Is this from the weight of the worlds he carries? Is that where he gains his strength? I wish I was the cotton that encircles his chest. Then, I could be closer to his heart. I could hear his rhythm, taste his sweat, and remind him of the beauty in his mass. I could know his body as intimately as he knows himself. His body, which I yearn to nourish and feed. The warm pillow I rest my head upon. The body that holds the stomach I admire. It is beautiful much like the rest of him.

Do you despise your temple like I despise mine? Have your insecurities become mirrors to you? Have you forgotten the root to "love handles"— love? They came to be from the love you've made to others. Do you wonder if they will stop you from making love with me? How do you feel in your jeans? Are you apprehensive to wear them? If so, you're not alone. Knowing that feeling is probably why I haven't stood up to approach you yet. If I told you how cloth accentuates your form, would you believe me? If I told myself the same thing, would I believe me? Let the worries exit your thoughts. I adore you.

I wonder what you smell like. I'm sure the scent of you could drive me wild. Your aroma would be my aphrodisiac. I yearn to be in your lap to inhale the very essence of you. Truly, the breath of life. And as your blood rushes and the warmth rises, I gaze into your eyes and coyly ask, "can I have it?" It's thick and glistens from your excitement. How does your sex feel? Do you wonder if you are sufficient? Do you ponder, "am I enough?" Silence your concerns.

I imagine your whimpers as you give me permission to your innermost places. The tops of your hips are the spots only few have been blessed to know. I'm a witness to your carnality: the arch in your spine, the way you

17

convulse, and how you quiver when touched. How trust has made you malleable. Your loss in the fight to conceal your groans. The copious essence emerging from your depths. Your permission to clasp the places you're most insecure. The release of your overwhelming strength. The grip of your legs that prevents my escape. The sounds and scents of our fluids mixing. The vocal eruption of your innermost feelings.

My mind races too quickly to "us". In ten seconds of stargazing, I've sped through ten years of union. I've arrived to a place where I've learned your language—your intonations and cadences. I've gathered how your body responds when you're tired, frustrated, ecstatic, and at peace. I've studied your honesty. I've witnessed your transparency and patience. Your resilience and your wholeness—your humanity.

How did I imagine so many occurrences in a matter of seconds? Why do I feel we could connect? Why am I afraid? I think it's because we're similar. We are hiding behind disguises we are slowly removing. I guess it's okay to be fearful of being "different". But I want to take this opportunity. To this man—I want to take off my mask with you.

Senses

What does it taste like?

I wonder how your sweat could nourish my taste buds. Your skin peppered with experience. My tongue savors you—your flavor.

What does it feel like?

How would you bend if my lips kissed the scars on your body? Lines that you're ashamed of. Marks that I adore. They guide me like paths that stretch across the land that I want to explore.

What does it smell like?

Your skin's aroma is yours alone. It changes when you're stressed. Relaxed. Aroused. The musk I crave exists where I often find myself—between flesh and hair. The place where your love resides. I inhale you deeply, my aphrodisiac.

What does it sound like?

Tell me how you feel in your body's language. Grumbles, gasps, words, curses, sighs, grunts. The sounds made when our bodies are moist, skin attached to skin.

What do you look like?

What do you think about when we arrive? What does your soul say when we peer into each other's eyes? The way your skin folds and your body glistens as you sweat. The way your hairs curve once I run my fingers through them. Our every insecurity vanishes for the moment. I've entered you. You reside in me. Inside each other completely.

Let's make fire forever, my love.

The Fire & The Rain

Infatuation is a very dangerous thing.

I don't understand why I love you the way that I do.

Many men captivated my eyes' attention, but only few have ensnared my mind, thus trapping my heart. My muse. The muse I can only claim in the depths of my mind. The muse who resides in one of the formerly vacant rooms of my heart's complex. You've made yourself at home, apparently. You feel comfortable...too comfortable.

I don't understand why I love you the way that I do.

I remember a time that I was jealous of you because you loved the man I admired from afar. Somehow, you and I became friends. It was like the rain yearning to touch the fire. Like flames outstretched and fighting to claim the sky. Only when they meet do they change form, affected by each other's presence. You were my rain. I was your fire.

I don't understand why I love you the way that I do.

The friendship evolved. Did the rain lust for heat? Is that what happened? What did I do to entangle you in a web that was meant for no one but myself? How did you wander to my light despite having your own? Why did you play with fire? Did the flames intrigue you because you knew something that the fire didn't—that rain doesn't burn? How do you know these things? What did you learn, rain? Did you see me reaching for the sky? I aimed for the clouds but, instead, I was greeted by you. Steam began to fill the air...

I've always been fascinated by the weather. I would look up and see you both happily floating. The rain and the light communing with other clouds in the sky. But you both have changed. Now you remind me of cumulonimbus clouds because I feel a storm is coming. I plead to you, "Please don't do this rain! I'll drown!"

Infatuation is a very dangerous thing.

I don't understand why you love me the way that you do.

He didn't see it from up there, but I already drowned. The sea of my infatuation dragged me to its depths. That ocean runs deep for this man who made a home in my mind. Who engraved his initials on my heart. I desire you in ways that even surprise myself. Your skin, the hue of nectarines, calls out to my tongue. What does your flesh taste like after marinating in your sweat? Could you feed me? The scars that caress your body are paths to the promised land. They follow the roundness of your figure and quickly form curves that I'm eager to explore.

What do your groans sound like? My mind races at the thought of our voices harmonizing in pleasure. How will you respond as the hairs of my beard crawl down your spine? Can we make love when the torrent pours and arrive at the same time the lightning crackles?

I don't understand why you love me the way that you do.

The steam fills the air. I think I've done the wrong thing. I shouldn't have been your introduction to warmth. You reassured me that this was your choice, but rain, you're dancing wildly in the wind. This storm is a mixture of your love and the cloud's tears. No matter how violently I set ablaze, I will never reach you because you live in the clouds. I don't have the heart to take you from the sky where you roam freely. This charred world, here on the ground that I burn, is not meant for you. Maybe you and the clouds will be fine. Leave me be that I may either dwindle away from fallen tears or choke from the dampened air.

I don't understand why you love me the way that you do.

Let me wander and let us love from afar. Rain, you will be mine in another lifetime. Live on. Sail in the ocean of the sky and I'll watch as you drift away.

Long Distance

You told me you couldn't do it again.
I shared the same with you.
But, after we met, has it crossed both our minds?

I remember the day I met you. You were visiting for business so your trip was going to be brief. I fantasized about the moment when my eyes would meet your gaze. I wondered what I would feel, how I would react, and how you would look. I was in awe that a man I've admired from afar was speaking with me in person. Laughing with me in the flesh. Exchanging time and energy with one another. You wore a fitted cap, a t-shirt, cargo shorts, and slides. You looked relaxed but I felt the tension in your spirit. Your nerves rattled you, but it was understandable.

We exchanged intimate moments with one another—stories of our experiences, our losses, and our growth. Then you asked if you could kiss me and I obliged. How could I not? I hungered for the taste of your lips well before you arrived. My mind raced as my eyes wandered around your body. Your skin was as radiant as your personality. Your tone fluctuated and revealed the depths of your tenderness. I traced the tattoo in the center of your chest with my tongue. I caressed the lines on your shoulders with my lips. I inhaled your scent deeply. I, willingly, crossed that line with you.

Why am I so enamored with you? Rather, how could I not be? You are a beautiful man inside and out. Your spirit is warm. You felt like heaven. At least what I hope heaven will be. A carnal force took over my body and allowed me to lose myself in your love. As I wandered, you moaned, "why are you doing this to me?" You uttered my name and asked, "does it taste good?" Oh, you gorgeous man, you could feed me for the remainder of my days. Bless me with all of you so I can pour myself into you.

I knew you had to leave soon. Much like the thunder and rain, the sunshine doesn't last forever. That's why I cherish those moments. You told me to buy some lottery tickets, as my luck struck a chord with you. I wasn't aware of that trait, nor do I play the lottery, but I bought them anyway because you requested it. As you drove away, I thought about our time together.

I missed you terribly as a I traveled back home from your hotel room. I yearned for your voice as the hours passed.

After that weekend, we conversed through phone calls and text messages. But it wasn't the same. I focused harder on my job and other responsibilities, only to learn how deeply embedded you were in my mind. Thoughts of you encircled me like longitudinal lines. That was the thing I feared most, yet equally desired.

You planted yourself in my heart. As memories take root, I feel the seeds of your presence growing quickly in the soil of my soul. Did you plan to do this? Or was it fate that brought us together? After meeting you, my perception of safety has changed. This man, who I'm much larger than, made me feel safe. Was it your voice? Was it your intellect? Or was it, simply, your touch? You've taught me so much in such a short time. Your hands were encompassed by mine, but my heart was ensnared by yours. You shined brilliantly like the warm Florida Sun. I now wonder— did God answer my questions?

You told me you couldn't do it again.
I shared the same with you.
But, after you left, has it crossed your mind?

I wonder if you would try long distance again...

Again

I wanna...

Feel butterflies
Look forward to texts and pillow talk
Play songs that make me think of you
Argue and fight, then forgive and learn
Always choose you
Support your dreams and goals
Protect and nurture you
Write poetry about you
Be safe with you
Cry with you
Hear you breathe
Know your morning and nightly routines
Fight for you
Adore your insecurities
Dance with you
Prepare your favorite food
Smell your fragrance on my t-shirt
Wish to father children with you
Place your hand in mine
Learn from you
Have you on my mind
Cool your heart
Feel you hold me
Listen to your heartbeat
Rest my head on your stomach
Make you feel young
Remind you of your beauty
Laugh at our inside jokes
Be your teammate
Share my last first kiss
Give you my final breath

...again.

Untitled

We have a funny relationship, you and I. It's distant sometimes. At other times, you're present.

You visit me every night to remind me of my worth. But when I wake, oftentimes, you're not there. Do you leave before the morning Sun? Is it because I start to long for the whole of you? Or because I crave parts of you in everyone else except you?

We have a funny relationship, you and I. Why must we play these games, Love?

*Imagine being
all three...*

LAMENTATION

My Bad

I spoke on manhood
It was fine 'til I came out
"You're gay, though?" ...my bad.

Is This Hell?

I don't know...

What if I'm already here? It's very hot...The voices in my mind grow louder and unbearable. Dull pain plagues me. My vision is deteriorating. The air is taken from me as I feel hands constrict my breathing while red tears, filled with my blood, run from my tear ducts.

If this is hell, I hope I make it through.

Why?

Why am I in a war that I never asked to be in?
Why am I fighting battles I'm sure I can't win?
Why does my hand tremble as I hold my blade?
Why do I continue forward when my spirit won't do the same?
Why do I embrace hope in my plea,
When I no longer carry that hope with me?

I don't know why.

I'm not afraid of not knowing why
I'm fearful that no living soul can give an answer that will suffice
I'm terrified that I'll never know the root of fruitless conflict
I'm mortified that insanity will gnaw at my conscious
My soul—bleed from me through my pen's ink
My brooding—relieve me from your plague, remove your stink
I write these words on bended knee as if I pray to my page
I weep my Black tears to process my Black rage
Am I the victim of attrition?
Why must I suffer from such conviction?
The more I learn, the more I ask—why are we doing this?
I've grown envious of the ignorant. I'm jealous of their bliss.

Bad Thoughts

I cannot trust you
You remind me of bad thoughts,
Your gaze and your voice.

Home

Home is not always full of love. Sometimes, it's filled with trauma. An aching pain that throbs the minute I begin my trek back there. I try to arrive slower while my thoughts race faster. I spend most nights in my bedroom crafting my resentment, all while playing music so my mind's pondering is hushed. At ease, my demons. I will entertain you soon enough.

Why is life like this? Why am I suffering? Will things get easier?

I ask these questions hourly knowing that an answer doesn't exist. Well, one that suffices more than "just have faith". It troubles me to admit that conviction is all I have. It means hoping for the future, not for the now. One day, I hope that faith fixes things. Until then, I really don't like being home.

Crucified

"I'm going to hell?!" – 13

My first thought after I realized the ones who crossed my mind were boys and men instead of girls and women.

"...I'm going to hell..." – 17

Raised in the Black church, molded in white Christian classrooms, I thought God didn't love me. How could he? He killed men who lusted for his angels. There's no way that he could love me...

"I'm...going to hell...?" – 19

No, I won't be going to hell...Not if I believe in someone else...right? God is wrong! The bible is wrong! It's ALL WRONG! I'm not an "abomination"! They didn't even use that damn word! Allah wouldn't treat me like this... would he?

"You're going to hell!!" – 19

Why would you say a demon is inside of me? Why are you mad at me?! Did I hurt you? Mama? Mama! MAMA?! Why have you forsaken me?!...why am I alive? Was it only to disappoint you? I'm so sorry...

"...you're...going to...hell..." – 19

"I...just because I'm attracted to men doesn't mean I can't have kids." It's strange to know that was the conversation that led to our demise. I guess I wasn't ready to lose my closest friend.

You didn't have to trick me into meeting your dad so he could minister to me. I should've saw it coming though, him being a pastor and all. You didn't have to invite me to the graduation ceremony at your mom's school. Especially if you knew the speaker would talk about men finding their God-ordained destiny. "Adam and Eve, not Adam and Steve"...I get it. You set me up, didn't you? Damn. You didn't have to give me a bible and say "this is just a phase that will pass." You could've just left me alone…

"You're going to hell…" – ∞

You're my dad, so I'm sure you love me. No need to reiterate. Though, I feel that if we had this conversation, you wouldn't love me anymore. You would tell me the same thing I've been hearing since I was 13. Maybe you really don't love me.

The New Normal

Imagination was my normal when I was a child. My action figures would wage epic quarrels with across their varied universes. My little warriors would equip their armor to defeat rogues and traitors. My biggest concern was having enough batteries to continue my never ending video game quests or to listen to jams I ripped and burned to CDs. My fears consisted of book reports, chemistry projects, or getting caught in the warm rain after playing basketball.

Summers were spent well as I was growing up. The minute I and my best friends learned how to drive, we frequented each other's houses just to freestyle to instrumentals or dance to songs crafted by young R&B phenoms (who were nothing more than teens more popular than us). We often drove up the street for fast food, feeling like adults with the world within our grasp. We knew what it was like to never have the internet. We also knew what it was like to explore this frightening new terrain. America, as well as the world, was online for the first time. I was building my own space through codes, backgrounds, and music playlists. I was learning things I wouldn't retain and playing video games...that was my normal. I was so happy then.

Things are different now. My happiness comes in short bursts and is afraid of longevity. I've lost many things...many people. Some of which I miss terribly. I've also gained new friends. Without them, I, too, would be of a lost generation. They say, as you get older, you get wiser. While that may be true, I think we get better at tricking ourselves to be happy. There's much to be joyous for. There's also much that reminds us that life isn't easy.

I often ask—

Why were you taken from me, my dearest uncle? My dearest Memama and Pepapa? Why did God, who claims to love us, choose to cause me eternal grief by taking you all from me?

God...why must we die? And I also must ask, why did you take my love away? He was a kind man. He loved me, and I him.

Why is loneliness a reality? Why has depression become my sibling who visits me more often than I want them to? Why do the thoughts of taking my own life plague me so? Why do I wander aimlessly, only to meander until it's my time to depart?

God—or whomever may be up there—why is this my new normal?

Martyrdom, a Cycle

Taught "don't talk back to your elders".
Learned "don't express feelings of discontent".
Reminded "enjoy them now because they won't always be here".
Internalizes feelings you were told to suppress.
Inflicts pain on one's self and others.
Have offspring.
Repeat.

La Muerte

I'm ready to blow my brains out

I've often thought about the way that I will die
After realizing the effort it takes to survive
How much strength it takes not to cry
When worlds burden my back and no answer to my "why?"
I've often thought about the way that I will die
I'm learning the difference between "living" and "alive"
I've often wondered what it would be like to be dead
When the voices leave and it's quiet in my head
Finally...

I'm ready to blow my brains out

The thought of taking my life if nothing new for me
I've actually grown comfortable with the idea
My death will happen in one of three ways
I'll decide which is best over glasses of sangria
Red as the blood that would exit my veins
As my life slowly drains from this vessel
I want it to be quick. I have nothing left
I've exhausted my strength with the demons I've wrestled
Devils, evil spirits haunt my mind's hallways
Their wails echo in the night
I fall further into their darkness, ensnared by their song
To befriend them seems easier than to fight
"Devil man, how can I help you take me?"
One of many questions I've asked
But, for some reason, he doesn't answer.
So, I wonder how long this will last

If I do not claim my life like I hoped to
Then my mind will slowly erode
Some beast, famished, will consume my memories
In my future, I will often say, "I don't know"

Or, "I don't remember...who are you?"
To my loved ones, I apologize in advance
I knew this would happen. I overworked myself
I've reached the end of my final dance
Please hold my hand as I leave this world
I'll smile as I feel your tears
My mother shared beautiful words about grief
"It's pent up love you wanna give to someone who's not here"
...that's if, I found love in the first place
The third of my deaths, the breaking of my heart
I've been there before and prefer not to revisit
There, the air was thin, so breathing was hard
I don't think I can endure that pain again
Crying myself to sleep, awaken to damp pillow cases
Suffering silently. Laughter is foreign to me
I would see you on everyone's faces
Happy without me, torturing me
Tuning my pain to your guitar's string
My tears cover you like sweat when you perform
My lamentation is the song you sing
Your stage presence inspired by my grief
I wept
Memories of what once was
I kept
As you lived, I fought to stay alive
I slept
But I did not wake from my slumber
I'm at rest

I'm ready to blow my brains out

I've often thought about the way that I will die
After realizing the effort it takes to survive
How much strength it takes not to cry
When worlds burden my back and no answer to my "why?"

I've often thought about the way that I will die
I'm learning the difference between "living" and "alive"
I've often wondered what it would be like to be dead
When the voices leave and it's quiet in my head
Finally...

...death.

Trust

I do not trust anyone because I do not trust *trust*. I'm lusted for, but I'm not valued. I offer the crumbs of my vulnerability for the world to consume while violently guarding the closest sections of my heart. Is this some twist of fate? Where I find solace in bringing my pain, plated on a custom salver, as an offering to their appetites? The flesh of my suffering satiates their hunger and I find peace in feeding the famished.

I've, unknowingly, built fortresses to protect myself. I believed each brick I removed allowed myself to be more transparent to the world. I didn't realize that I didn't remove those obstructions, but repurposed them for more intricate defenses. Systems were created that even I was unaware of. Was it second nature? Maybe I knew to protect myself prior to knowing my enemy. Maybe I knew to protect myself from me.

This is why I don't trust. Or, maybe I do trust, but only myself. I think this is because I've learned to create shelters for my spirit while cautiously trickling the contents of my heart. I heal by sharing these feelings. Feelings that are as food for your well-being, which confirms that we, both, are not alone in our suffering.

Love v. Like

True, you do love me,
You just don't like me, do you?
...Well, I'm not surprised.

Mirrors

I was always self-conscious. I always worried that you would leave me for someone who was smaller than me. In a roundabout way, you did. I'm constantly reminded of him—well, them—when I walk into my therapy meetings. Their waists are thin unlike mine.

You liked the men who made me feel inadequate. Those men were the popular boys in high school because they had abs, muscles, and were considered "fine". They weren't particularly strong, but they were particularly mean. In hindsight, it was petty high school shit, but it stuck with me.

I never thought I was good enough to receive love, let alone affection. At one point, you liked bigger men like me. Now, you don't...or, not as much as you claimed you did. Truthfully, I don't know. I only know that, these days, I wouldn't be your first choice. I thought if I could support you, learn to cook so I could feed you, heal you when you were sick, be stronger so I could protect you, wiser so I could fight for you, be more eloquent and accomplished so you could brag about me...I thought if I did all of those things, I would be enough. But, as it turns out, I wasn't.

The mirror constantly reminds me that I wasn't sufficient. Maybe I won't ever be ample for you or for anyone else. I'm scared to accept that, but maybe I have to. I was and will never be enough. Not for you, at least. The mirror tells me all of these truths.

Size Matters

He said, "you're bigger than I expected!"
I said, "Thanks."

He said, "...you're bigger than I expected..."
I said, "...thanks?"

Untitled

The three most common insults I've received:
Nigger, faggot, and fat.

Imagine being all three.

*One day, I hope to
not cry so much...*

LIBERATION

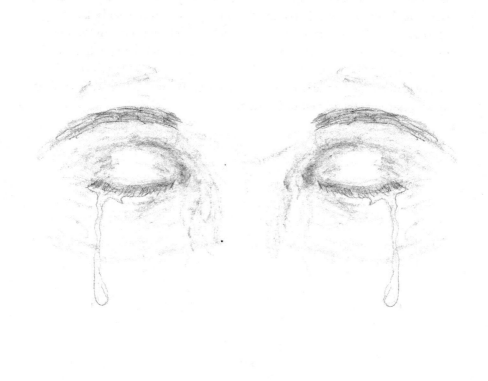

Stars

I wonder if the stars were brighter 100 years ago. Less toxins and pollution blocked our vision. But, then again, maybe the sky was always dark for us, especially our ancestors. It's ironic how we both would dream our wildest as we gazed at Orion's belt.

I dreamt of days where I could love and live. They dreamt of days where they could live and love. I dreamt of running wildly in the fields, laughing. They dreamt of running away from the fields, anxiously. I dreamt of my depression receding. They dreamt of their oppression leaving. I dreamt of days where I could wear my smile. They dreamt of days where they could worry less for their child. In this dark sky with dimly lit stars, we looked up and we both wildly dreamt of freedom.

Untitled

I cry a lot.

One day, I hope to not cry so much.
I'd like to cry a little less.
I pray that day is coming soon.
Much sooner than I expect.

Smiles

I've met many men with beautiful smiles. Laughter that's filled with relief from their pain. Eyes lit brightly, despite the many tears they've cried in the dark. Mouths that have spoken truths and have told lies to protect themselves. It's astounding because there are so many stories and reasons why they smile. Through their hurt, their frustrations, their fears...

I'm glad to have met you in this lifetime. Though, my heart is fearful to give itself to you. Maybe we both crave affection, but deep down we know that we want other people...and my heart is okay with that. Regardless, I'm glad I've given you a reason to smile. We've shared our pain and our hope with each other. I leave you with one final request:

Smile, oh you beautiful man, smile!

Dedicated to P███a, N██o, and M███o

Freedom

I want freedom,
But what is it that I want to be free from?
I want to be freed from systems that keep me trapped
Insecure about my dialect, my inflections, my Black

I want the freedom to not be ashamed of my ways
From the pressure of numbering and counting down my days
Freedom, I want my mind to finally be at ease
And self-harm, self-deprecation, and self-hate just leave

I want to be free from the lens that covers my eyes
And makes me despise my reflection, then look for a disguise
That makes me feel good until I can get home and cry
And accept I can only walk because I'm too heavy to fly

I want freedom, for kids whose weight we've chastised
Because they grow up to be like me, afraid to see a pant size
Or they grow up to be mean, play on sports teams,
Then bully and target the kids who didn't want to be seen

I want freedom, from my trauma that spans generations
I want freedom, but I'm exhausted in this fight for liberation
It's frustrating, most of the time I feel defeated
Because they see us mistreated and still won't believe it

I want my right to be human, the ability to be me
In every aspect. I want the liberty to be.

I want freedom.

Out East

The evening was warm.

Warm enough for sweat to coat my skin. The rough smell of nicotine brushed against my nostrils as I brought bags of groceries into Uncle Ruben's house. I did my best not to inhale because it messes with my sinuses. The Sun was drifting off to slumber, but its presence lingered for a little bit longer. Small, old homes line the streets of the Eastside, better known as "out East" if you're from these parts.

Houses filled with Black pain and perseverance. Black remorse and resilience. Brown skin glistens while the grass is watered, while the soil is tilled, on the trek to the corner store, sitting out on the porch watching time go by. Watching time go "bye". Your family's roots were planted here as you branched throughout the city. You remember these homes well. You know this feeling of familiar. Liquor stores and Church's or Popeyes' Chicken are staples to the 'hood. It's something special. You may live somewhere else, but you'll never forget where you come from.

Many images appear in my head when I think about Out East. I remember my Memama and Pepapa's house so clearly. It was a small home with doors on two sides of the house, parallel to each other. One door closest to the garage in the back. The other closest to the porch and the street they lived on—East 25th. I remember walking through the back door and stepping into a small brown room to the right. When my cousin lived there, I used to sneak into his room and play his Playstation when he was at work. To the left was the bathroom. Light green wallpaper with tiny pink roses in vertical columns graced the walls. The gas heater made it a little cramped as I got older and, subsequently, bigger.

From there, I would walk right into the kitchen. Golden yellow wallpaper with white stripes and reddish-brown cabinets filled this room. To the left were the sink, the window peering out into the yard, and the dull green gas stove. She used to work miracles on that stove. My first time having catfish was in this kitchen. To this day, no catfish can compare. Centered nicely was a round dinner table with a decorative plastic table skirt, circled by three chairs. To the right were the off-white fridge, a stand that held the microwave and boxes of plain crackers, and a medium-sized heater with a TV on top. That TV, with temperamental antennas, was good for background noise when Memama cooked and I finished my homework. But it was never on when Memama or Pepapa had to, as they would say, get their lesson. That was their bible study space.

To the right of the kitchen was the entryway to Memama's room. She had a beautiful dresser filled with her make-up, lots of jewelry, and other things she cherished. There was always some candy around. My favorites were the Werther Original's and the red candies in the strawberry wrappers. She always had a carrying case for her bible so she could organize her notes. I remember the blue circular tin that was filled with sewing supplies instead of the cookies that it advertised. The large and comfortable mattress sat nicely on the dark wooden bedframe and with beautiful bedding. Next to it was her window that looked out into the driveway. She had cable in her room, so I often stayed in there.

Going through the doorway from the kitchen was the living room. Columns of light brown wood caressed the walls, with two couches on the left and right sides of the room. In the center was a long, but low wooden table that was always topped with newspaper articles. There were small drawers underneath it that revealed tons of magazines they read over the years. Pepapa loved reading the paper when he wasn't watching baseball games. If my memory serves me right, there was a tall clock rested in the corner of the living room. To the right was the doorway to Pepapa's room. It was much lighter in color than Memama's. His bed was much firmer as well. I remember his dresser full with stacks of envelopes tied with rubberbands. I think Pepapa's bible was a warm cherry, almost the color of red wine.

And out of the living room was the porch which faced the houses across the street. Welded onto the gate was Pepapa's name, "C. James". The same gate that surrounded the beautiful garden they grew and cared for. A thick oak tree was encompassed by plants and flowers in every color of the spectrum. The grass was watered almost every other day, I believe. So the yard was always lush, healthy, and vibrant. My visits became less and less since they aren't home anymore. Uncle Ruben lives there now and keeps things in order as best as he can. Now, my visits have become more frequent. Not only for Uncle Rubin's sake, but also for mine. I understand and appreciate things differently now that I'm older. There's a feeling that carves itself into the pit of your stomach when you return to a place from which you came. The feeling, made up of memories and experiences, sits and waits until you decide to acknowledge it. That's what brings me back out East.

The evening was warm.

Warm enough to muster fears and agitation in your heart. The heat of Florida summers never seems to subside. A lot can happen in a hot house. A lot of good and a lot of bad. It took a while before I understood why folks sit outside. They need a break from the thoughts their homes force them to reckon with. The voices they hope to silence. The white noise they hope to fill with something...anything. Anything but those thoughts.

Warm Southern breezes flow through the empty lots filled with moths and butterflies, empty Colt 45 cans, brewsky bottles, worn down tires, and weeds. The sounds of crickets harmonize with the cicadas and grasshoppers. Around 7pm is when the sky is saturated with orange rays—evening time. That's when it's the most beautiful out on the porch. It's something about out East that keeps me grounded to the Earth. This connection to my ancestors who saw that same 7pm sunlight. Hot summer evenings, their skin glowing, and sitting on the porch watching time go by. Watching time go, "bye".

The evening was warm,...out East.

Going to Work

We all call my grandma, "Momma", and she works in a hospital. Specifically, she's worked in the IT department for 29 years. I was born in that hospital shortly after she started working there. I remember her and my mom worked multiple jobs. When my mom was at work, I would go to that hospital when Momma worked her 3–11pm shift.

She worked alongside many co-workers, plenty who have faded from my memory. We took the first floor elevator down to the basement, then walked down long hallways until we made it to her work area. They weren't that long, but that's hard to explain to a 9-year-old. There were really big printers, each churning out sheets upon sheets of data from the hundreds of computers that surrounded us.

I recall walking through the office door. To the right were pipes leading above and below, neatly contained in the indention of the wall. To my immediate left was a door that lead to a hallway-like room with workstations, including hers. Straight ahead led to a room with columns of computer towers and printers. I think they were a faint green, while the floor was tiled with white squares. I always wondered if there was a secret code if I stepped on the correct sequence of panels. A little further in the room, the floor was raised about six inches from the ground. This is where the big printers were. The sounds of data processing, machines typing code onto paper, and fans keeping these leviathans comfortable was addicting. In hindsight, I assume that's what my young brain sounded like. Maybe it sounds like that today.

As a young artist, my mind was overflowing with ideas. Momma would give me reams of paper and I drew countless stories that, now, escape my memory. The paper was strange. It had transparent green and white rows where text would normally be printed. It was perforated and those margins had holes punched in them. It reminded me of the scan-tron paper I filled in when taking those asinine tests in school. During these times, I wasn't limited to #2 pencils and multiple choice bubbles. I was free to roam the paper to my heart's content.

I remember going to the cafeteria on the first floor. The food wasn't particularly stellar, but I enjoyed it. There was something special about the styrofoam cups covered in funky green, blue, and purple brush stroke designs. As an adult, I deeply cherish these moments. I always went to work with Momma.

As we've both gotten older, things changed. Funny enough, we've both visited that hospital as patients. Momma walks with a cane now, constantly in pain from her knee surgery. The office changed as well. It was relocated down the hall with more streamlined technology. New employees, a new floor plan, and all without the sounds I grew accustomed to. Now, it's the sounds of keyboards clicking and phones constantly ringing. I've been able to learn her morning routine with her early weekend shifts: After she signs in, she gets her mug from the drawer above her computer and fixes a cup of coffee using the office Keurig—one cycle to fill up a medium-sized cup, reset the timer, then one cycle to fill up a small-sized cup, topped off with a bit too much creamer.

She brings her own creamer and water for the Keurig, but sometimes it's too heavy for her. It wasn't like that twenty years ago. My God...so much has happened in twenty years. Nowadays, I make her lunch and walk her to the office. As she slowly hobbles to her workstation, I put her food in the brown mini-fridge, ask for her mug, then I get her coffee ready. I no longer stay with her at work. Instead, I wish her a good day, hug and kiss her, tell her "I love you", then I head home to sleep a bit before I pick her up.

One morning, I realized that I'm, now, the one who helps take care of her. It saddens me because the older we grow, the sooner she'll leave me. I try to cherish these moments every time I have them. This hospital has much history—my birth, her workplace, and where I fought for my life only a few short years ago. Truthfully, the hospital has always been a part of my life.

Something I'll never forget is what she shared with me when I was in high school. She said, "you're never ashamed of your ol' grandma. Some other kids would be embarrassed, but you never tried to hide me." Admittedly,

I thought to myself, "well, you can get a little loud, but I really love you." How could I be ashamed? You've been with me my whole life. I've learned as much from you as I've learned from my mother. Thank you for birthing and rearing her. You blessed me with the greatest gift.

And thank you for always taking me to work with you, Momma.

Nephew

I remember the first time I saw you draw. I was fascinated! You captured my mind and had no intentions of letting me go. You drew a lot of characters in still poses. Nothing too dynamic. But, to me, the ink came alive on the paper. You brought life to your ideas and they gazed at the viewer with soul and intent. Pictures of your characters were pinned and taped to your cornflower blue wall beside your colorful *WordUp! Magazine* posters. You inspired me to learn how to draw.

But then you stopped.

Or maybe I was too busy with homework to see any new ideas you worked on. Did anyone believe in your creative voice? Or, rather, did your father believe in your creative voice? Your sister and Momma saw it. We all saw your gift. Did you, unknowingly, pass your talents down to me? Or was I so fixated on being like you that it happened naturally?

I remember when we went to Blockbuster to rent video games. I remember you said, "ask Momma if we can get the Sega Saturn. She'll rent it if *you* ask." I was against it because I wanted the Sony Playstation, but I asked anyway. And, sure enough, she did. We played "Virtua On" and "Virtua Fighter". You introduced me to fighting games—specifically, Street Fighter 2. It's funny how that stuck with me for over 20 years. Thank you.

I remember a lot about you. Your homies, your girlfriends...a good handful of them. Some of them I love to this day. Others, I'd rather forget than recall. My best friends loved you, but not as much as me. That's because you were mine and I was yours. My uncle, your nephew. Always.

You always supported me. Everybody in the 'hood knew you and, therefore, knew me. Countless times I've heard, "You don't remember me. You was little back then!" They were right. Out of the many friends I do remember, there are twice as many that don't ring a bell. How wonderful it is to know the effect you had on people. Everybody knew me as "Thad's nephew". Before, I used it to navigate unfamiliar places. Now, I wear it as a badge of honor.

I always wanted to show you the new fighting games that came out. I remember you said you wanted to play ball with me. We never got around to it, and that's okay. I was just happy to see you, even though we grew a little distant. Looking back, we did so much together. You saw so many of my accomplishments and I would always think, "I made him proud! I bet he's telling his friends about me..." I remember being in the airport that Friday morning, finally reading the article I was featured in. I was so excited and couldn't wait to show you when I came back in town.

Then God called you home...

...God called you home.

God...why did you take him from me? Why would you hurt me like this?! Do you hate me?! Did I do something wrong? I just...I hate you right now. I didn't get to tell him my good news...He was supposed to be there and you took him from me! I hate you so much right now...fuck...

Time has not healed this wound. I miss you every single day. Oftentimes, I wonder if I'll ever be happy again. When I was returning home, I felt your presence on my flight. I saw you in the beautiful valleys of clouds and, instead of playing ball, we flew and saw heaven together. As I descended, you ascended, both of us headed home. Your legacy was, unknowingly, left with me. And, like I've done before, I will make you proud.

I can hear you, as clear as day, telling me, "Love ya, neph!" Thank you for gracing me with your presence and leaving your eternal mark engraved on my heart. Thank you for giving me the gifts you once possessed. Thaddeus, I love you. Forever and always.

Your nephew.

When I Grow Up

What do you want to be when you grow up?

"I want to be a chef!"

I remember when you were finishing your culinary arts program. Your class prepared meals and desserts for everyone to try. You were moving at the speed of lightning, but I'll always remember your chef's hat and jacket. That was the night I decided the rest of my life by wanting to be a chef. Years later, I saw you cater party after party, event after event, cook in local kitchens, and onward to the Olympics. I just knew I'd be a chef after seeing you in action! Truthfully, that dream didn't come about, but I learned how to prepare and have a deeper appreciation for food.

"I want to be a meteorologist!"

I've always been fascinated by the weather. After my father left, there were many evenings you cried and slept until it was time for you to go to your job at the time. You worked the night-shift, so I would get my toys, clothes, and video games together before you dropped me off at Momma's house. While you were sleeping, I would peep into your room and whisper, "I love you". Then, I would find myself in the living room watching movie re-runs, never-ending cycles of weather news, and episodes of tornado-loving amateur storm chasers before it was a tv series. Hurricanes are formed over warm bodies of water, while tornadoes are birthed from warm and cool air pressure colliding into each other. Maybe I learned the weight of your tears at the same time. I witnessed how storms are created and the devastation they leave behind.

My love of storms inspired me to watch the news as I got ready for school in the mornings. I'd watch for all sorts of weather activity. I even had favorite meteorologists after a while. Eventually, I learned that science wasn't my favorite nor strongest subject. My hopes of being a meteorologist were cut short, but I've learned to weather the literal and metaphorical storms that have come my way.

"I want to be an artist!"

Through all of my aspirations, art has always been at my side. I drew any and everything I could. Every video game, action figure, and trading card you bought me were subject to my own artistic interpretation. I had notebooks and folders filled with stories and original characters. Drawing was the tip of the iceberg.

As a child, I didn't understand the directions you pushed me towards. Band practice, piano lessons, and learning karate, to name a few. Now, as an adult, I can't thank you enough for these opportunities. I wasn't the best at playing the trumpet, nor was I the strongest pianist nor highest ranking martial artist. Though these experiences taught me the lessons you needed me to understand early in life—try my hardest and never give up.

I remember when you bought me a condenser microphone to start up my budding recording studio. You were hesitant on the purchase. Rightfully so, as the microphone, the mixer, and the additional parts totaled an (at the time) astronomical number. But what an investment it turned out to be! Little did we both know that my creativity expanded beyond the visual and into the audible. Through music, I learned to dream wildly and to chase after those dreams as hard as I could.

I left for New York when I was 21. In my mind, I felt I was ready for graduate school. In my heart, I took that leap of faith for a lover at the time. In my soul, I felt so much pain as I left the nest to spread my wings. That time was extremely hard. To leave everything I knew for a world I couldn't truly prepare for. There were so many nights I regretted my decision and wished I could come back home. But, somehow, you trusted me. In some way, you forced yourself to stay back and let me find my way. I created a gash in your heart that I still regret. No one wants to hurt their mama. I hope the life I've lived and the work I've made thus far has culminated into an acceptable apology.

You believed in me more than anyone could ever hope to attempt. Every lesson you taught me, both through example and through experience, helped me survive one of the hardest moments of my journey thus far. And, even now, I still have the letter you wrote for me before I boarded that plane. You raised me well.

I remember when my world crumbled in my hands. My former lover left me. There were so many nights I cried myself to sleep and woke up in tear drenched pillows. I drowned in the sorrows of my own hurricane. As I wallowed in the wreckage, you spoke with the sternness of a captain who has sailed those waters before. You, my super woman, saved me from the darkest corners of my mind. I owe my life to your prayers. And through living, I've created works of art that will last beyond my lifetime.

You are the greatest gift I've been blessed with. There aren't enough words in any language to explain my adoration, admiration, and gratitude. It would take me a million lifetimes to gather enough words that can articulate how much I love you. We've been through so much together. From being with you as you worked two, three, and too many jobs to sitting beside you in your evening college classes, I'm blessed to witness you. I'm privileged to learn from you. I'm honored to be of you.

What do you want to be when you grow up?

I want to be just like you, Mama. I love you.

One Day, I Hope That...

I.

One day, I hope that...

My worries will no longer trouble me. I look forward to the days where the pieces of my mind find comfort in their reconstruction. I pray for those days that God so sparingly distributes, like pieces of the sweetest candy. Days where I can just be. Days filled with hours that I can claim as my time: to know me better, to love and reassure me, and simply to be *me*.

In my time, I want to lay in my bed; I want to daydream of climbing smoky mountains to slay dragons, only to befriend them so I could gain their wisdom; fantasize of racing through moonlit forests on life or death missions with my fellow shinobi, only to exchange shuriken, kunai, and katanas with those from an enemy village; imagine myself enchanting an audience with verbal incantations I've refined through my years of creative writing; envisioning a studio of canvases and pages filled with incomplete thoughts, unfinished ideas, and explorations of color and the human form, only to find more paper to draw and tell stories to my heart's content.

In my time.

II.

You'll find out I'm gay if you read this. You'll probably hate me and blame my "condition" on my mother. You'll probably say, "If I was there, this wouldn't have happened". It would have.

You'll exile me from your side of the family. Well, you did that when I was 9, so this is familiar territory. Tell your mom I grew my hair out and it's lovely. You know, because she always had slick comments about me not getting a haircut.

Remember those times you invited me to holiday gatherings and celebrations? Where I forced conversation and played the Oscar-worthy role of the son aching for acceptance? There were two things, among many, that were wrong: First, you didn't want the wholeness of me to attend. Just the image of success that you want to falsely associate yourself with. Second, this was never a home for me to come back to. But tell your family I said "hello".

You'll probably confront me and threaten me. I'm not worried about that. I'll cross that bridge when it's time to.

You'll probably think, "this ain't no son of mine". It is.

You'll probably say, "I don't know if I can love you anymore". It's fine. I never believed you liked me, so I knew you could stop loving me. You never believed in me. Just believe every word that I wrote.

III.

To my mother,

I love you.

I love you to the end of time itself. My gratitude for you can cause the seven seas to overflow. You frustrate me, true. And I'm sure I frustate you. But I would never replace you. I am honored to be one of your greatest accomplishments. I am blessed to know you and to come from you.

To my mother and my number one girl,

I love you to the Moon and back.

IV.

I am my brother's keeper. To you, my brother,

You have rescued me from death's embrace time and time again. I will
protect you until my dying breath. My spirit will cloak your heart and soul
forever and a day. I will teach you to protect your light for when I'm no
longer here. I'm sorry for any pain or disappointment I've caused you. I will
help lift the burdens you bear. I will celebrate your freedom as the world
tries to confine you.

Black boy. Brown skin. Angel. Thrive in your joy! You are more than what
men say you are. You are *you!* I celebrate you. I hold hands with you. I love
you. Black boy. Brown-skinned Angel. You are magnificent. You are worthy.
You are enough.

I am my brother's keeper. To you, my brother,

I love you.

V.

I love you, Black girl.

To Black girls,
Tall Black girls,
Short Black girls,
Fat Black girls,
Thick Black girls,
Skinny Black girls,
Muscular Black girls,
Queer Black girls,
Trans Black girls,
Straight Black girls,
Cis Black girls,
Nerdy Black girls,
Ghetto Black girls,
Bougie Black girls,
Bisexual Black girls,
Genderfluid Black girls,
Multiracial Black girls,
Dark skin-toned Black girls,
Brown skin-toned Black girls,
Light skin-toned Black girls,
Black girls with disabilities,
Differently-abled Black girls,
Poor Black girls,
Loud Black girls,
Quiet Black girls,
Soft-spoken Black girls,
Awkward Black girls,
Self-conscious Black girls,
Confident Black girls,
Wealthy Black girls,
Black girls who smile,

Black girls who don't smile,
Black girls who've had their smiles taken from them,
Masculine Black girls,
Feminine Black girls,
Black girls who went to school
Black girls who didn't go to school
Angry Black girls
Sad Black girls
Happy Black girls
Depressed Black girls
Anxious Black girls
Black girls in sex work
Black girls who cry,
Black girls who weren't allowed to cry,
Black girls who are survivors,
Black girls who we've lost,
All Black girls,
Every Black girl,
You are enough. You are worthy. You are a blessing. You are loved. You deserve happiness.

I love you.

VI.

To the boys and men who...

Didn't play, don't play, or don't like sports
Are socially awkward at times
Don't feel comfortable in their skin
Are pressured to be leaders when they would rather follow
Don't have it all together
Are queer, bisexual, gay, trans, and any gender identity
Are shy
Don't feel "man enough"
Don't have "ideal" or "perfect" bodies
Come in every shape and size
Are scared
Are gentle and soft-spoken
Love to read books, paint pictures, bake cakes
Love to dance, do make-up, tell stories, and write poetry
Cry
Are self-conscious of their bodies
Cope with performance anxiety
Are feminine
Are emotional
Crave affection from their friends
Smile in person and in pictures
Don't smile in person and pictures because they weren't allowed to
Are figuring out what life means
Don't live up to their family's or society's expectations of them
Are told "that's not what boys and men do"
Want or need help, but are told to "man up"
Keep trying, even when the odds are against them

...you are enough.

I love you.

VII.

Present You, Future You,

Have you found love yet?
With a partner? With yourself? If you haven't, that's okay.
Keep searching. It will happen.

Have you checked on yourself?
Have you cooled your heart so you may listen to what it has to say? Have
you communed with time to reflect on the days and seconds that have long
left us? I think you should. Seeing our reflections does good for us.

Have you smiled lately? Your laughter is infectious. I miss hearing it. Don't
you?

Remember to speak kindly to yourself.
Continue to believe.
Believe in yourself and your joy.
Have faith in your worth.
You're reading this because you've made it this far.
Keep going.

I'm rooting for you, beloved.

ACKNOWLEDGEMENTS

First and foremost, all praise to the Most High. This body of work would not have come to fruition if it wasn't for You. I'm eternally grateful for the many blessings You've given me, as well those that are in the future. I learned faith through You.

To my brothers—Chris, Brian, Phil, Caleb, Luis, Makaio—you all are cherished beyond all belief. Larry, thank you for your friendship, brotherhood, and for your creative vision. Our connection to one another is what keeps me yearning to understand myself more. I will always love and cherish the artwork you crafted for this book. You all are angels.

To my family—especially my mother, my grandmother, and my brother— thank you. Your love for me is limitless. I love you well into my next lifetimes.

To my extended family—words cannot express my gratitude for you all. I shared both my loss and my truth, and you embraced me with open arms and open hearts. Jacinda, Carlos, Aldrena, George, Nakita, Douglas, Gaby, Dian, Jessica, Terresa, Phim, Andrew, Lucy, Sue, & Julie—thank you. Rich, your words still echo in my heart. You are a wonderful man, a wonderful human, and a wonderful father. I'm honored to know you, my friend. Thank you.

To my muses—your influence and inspiration cannot be understated. Thank you for filling my heart with feelings and my mind with ponderings of the future. We exchanged sweet nothings, only for some of you to go your separate ways. Despite this, I'm grateful for the moments we created. They guided me to this place where I strive for honesty. Through you all, I learned many facets of infatuation, attraction, and love.

To all of you wonderful souls, thank you.

One Day, I Hope That...

Scan here to visit marqmervin.com

About Marq

Marq Mervin is a multifaceted artist, designer, educator, and author based in Jacksonville, Florida. He is also an advocate of art and design education for marginalized and underrepresented communities. During his downtime, Marq is either gaming or performing poetry at open mic nights.

Scan here to listen to the single
"One Day I Hope That"
on streaming platforms

#ODIHT

CPSIA information can be obtained
at www.ICGtesting.com
Printed in the USA
LVHW042238210920
666689LV00024B/1021